D0332243

# Slavery in Ancient Egypt and Mesopotamia

# Slavery in Ancient Egypt and Mesopotamia

**Jacqueline Dembar Greene**

**Watts** LIBRARY

**Franklin Watts**
A Division of Grolier Publishing
New York • London • Hong Kong • Sydney
Danbury, Connecticut

**Note to readers:** Definitions for words in **bold** can be found in the Glossary at the back of this book.

Photographs ©: Bridgeman Art Library International Ltd., London/New York: 31, 9 (PHD31193/Tomb of Menna; harvest sequence. Wall painting, c. 1400 BC. Chicago Press, USA), 26 (SCP65163/Hammurabi, king of Babylon, praying before a sacred tree. c. 1750 BC. Bronze and gold. Louvre. Paris, France), 29 (LOU69506/'Code of Hammurabi': the god Shamash dictating his laws to Hammurabi, King of Babylon, Mesopotamian, found at Susa, Iran. c. 1750 BC. Diorite, height :225 cm. Louvre. Paris, France); Corbis-Bettmann: 48 (Richard T. Nowitz), 6 (Baldwin H. & Kathryn C. Ward); North Wind Picture Archives: 5, 10, 11, 12, 16, 23, 32, 33, 43; Panos Pictures: 21 (Daniel O'Leary); Stock Montage, Inc.: 35, 36, 37, 44, 50; Superstock, Inc.: 20, 49 (Bridgeman Art Library, London/Private Collection), 38 (Silvio Fiore), 19 (Silvio Fiore/Museum of Baghdad, Baghdad, Iraq), 40, 46 (Jewish Museum, New York), 42; The Art Archive: 24.

Cover illustration by Carol Werner.

Visit Franklin Watts on the Internet at:
http://publishing.grolier.com

**Library of Congress Cataloging-in-Publication Data**

Greene, Jacqueline Dembar.
    Slavery in Ancient Egypt and Mesopotamia / by Jacqueline Dembar Greene
        p. cm.— (Watts Library)
    Includes bibliographical references and index.
    Summary: Follows the course of slavery in Mesopotamia and Egypt, examining how this practice began and spread, the work slaves did, and the impact of slavery on ancient societies.
    ISBN 0-531-11692-1 (lib. bdg.)    0-531-16538-8 (pbk.)
1. Slavery–Egypt–History–Juvenille literature. [1. Slavery–Egypt–History. 2. Slavery–Iraq–History–To 634.] I. Title. II. Series.
HT1371 .G73 2000
—dc21
                                              00-038196

# Contents

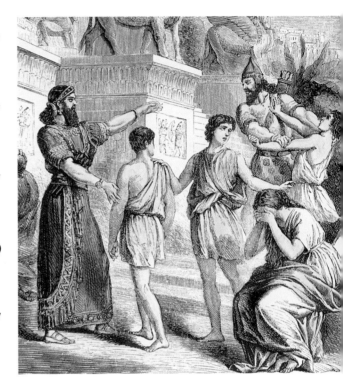

The lives of slave women often involved hard labor.

## Chapter One

# How Slavery Began

No one knows exactly when slavery began, but it was part of many societies from the earliest times. Slavery is a system in which people own other people. Typically, slaves are treated as objects, rather than human beings, and are considered to be inferior to their owners. The owner can require any type or amount of work from a slave, rent the

## Slavs to Slaves

The word *slave* comes from the name of a group of people called Slavs who lived in Eastern Europe. The name *Slav* originally meant "glory." Between the fifth and thirteenth centuries A.D., Germans and other groups invaded Slavic lands and captured and sold so many people that the meaning of the word changed. Europeans used the word *slave* to mean any person held in **bondage**.

slave's labor, or sell him or her. Slaves are denied the right to make decisions about their own lives.

In ancient times, many free people became slaves because they were captured and enslaved during wars. Also, some people sold themselves, or their children, to a wealthy person in order to pay off their debts. Sometimes, a man who couldn't provide for his family became a rich man's slave in return for food, clothing, housing, and protection.

Occasionally, large groups of people moved to a new land for safety or for better farmland. They might have offered to work for the ruler in return for permission to live in his country.

## The First Slaves

Many historians believe that farming led to the development of slavery. In the earliest times, people were **nomads**—they moved from one place to another, hunting animals and gathering wild food. Later, people settled in one area and grew their own crops. Soon they needed more workers. Before these permanent settlements, soldiers usually killed their ene-

mies. After farming became a way of life, the victorious army realized that they could use captives as free labor. The conquering rulers of Mesopotamia made slaves of defeated soldiers and civilians, or sold them for profit. Later, the pharaohs of Egypt relied on slaves as palace workers and as labor for building roads, monuments, and aqueducts.

With slave labor, people could farm larger pieces of land and grow more crops. They could store extra grain for use during lean times and sell their surplus. The early farmers who used slaves didn't feel that they were mistreating them. They reasoned that if the captives hadn't been sold, they would have been killed. Enslaving defeated enemies seemed kinder than

*This wall painting shows slaves farming the harvest.*

9

*Slaves helped erect the public buildings in cities.*

killing them. When a man owned slaves, he didn't think of them as people. Instead, he felt as if he had another ox or donkey to serve his needs. Just as an ox pulled a plow, a slave planted seeds.

Slaves were also used in households to do the work needed to make their masters' lives comfortable. They ground grain, cooked and baked food, served meals, and cleaned the houses. The slaves even made the clothing that their owners wore.

When early societies realized that it could be profitable, slavery increased. Those who could afford it bought more and more land and needed more and more slaves to cultivate it.

Convicted criminals and **debtors** who couldn't repay money they owed were no longer sent to prison. Instead, the courts sentenced them to forced labor, working for the state. They built roads, worked in mines, and did other hard and dangerous jobs. As villages grew into cities, more public projects were needed, and the demand for workers increased. Soon wars were fought just to capture prisoners for slave labor.

## A Matter of Fate

Slavery was common in every country in ancient times. Skin color did not matter. Masters and slaves came from all races, and some people enslaved members of their own tribes and cultures.

People realized that becoming a slave depended on the outcome of a battle, and often on sheer luck. Many people believed that an individual's position in life was the will of the

*This woodcut shows a slave owner punishing a slave while other slaves look on.*

gods. The gods decided whether a person would be rich or poor, healthy or sick, and a person could do nothing to change it. Slavery was just one possible situation in life. People didn't consider it to be wrong or as something that needed to be corrected. If the gods willed it, a person had to accept his fate. Centuries later, this thinking carried over to newly discovered lands in North and South America. Invading armies from European countries defeated the native people and often enslaved them.

Even the early **philosophers**, educated men who wrote and spoke about their ideas of truth and values, also believed that slavery was part of the natural order of life. They encouraged slaves to be obedient and advised masters to be firm.

These thinkers never considered freeing slaves. Only two early groups of Hebrews spoke out against slavery, but they were a small minority in their time.

Permanent settlements grew into larger **city-states**, which consisted of a large city and its surrounding territory under one strong government. In a larger population, more people had to work for others to earn a living. Not every family could own land and grow enough food to support itself. Life became more complicated. More food was needed, and people wanted more goods and services. Slaves became a large part of the workforce. To provide the labor, a slave trade developed across a wide area. Slavery was one of the earliest forms of commerce between people and nations.

Some men grew wealthy through their landholdings and eventually owned hundreds, or thousands, of slaves. Many slaves worked at hard labor, such as construction and mining. Others were allowed to use their education or special skills to tutor an owner's children or to entertain. Slaves eventually worked in every type of job that a developing civilization needed, including doctors, librarians, weavers, jewelers, soldiers, carpenters, and chefs. Growing city-states came to depend upon slave workers to maintain their way of life.

## What Was a Slave Worth?

Although they might be expensive to buy, slaves were thought of as property, like an animal or a tool. Owners didn't usually worry about working a slave to exhaustion, or even to death.

This was particularly true of slaves working on large agricultural estates or in government mines. If a slave died, the owner simply bought a new one.

As more slaves did the difficult jobs and fewer owners worked at all, a sharper division arose between the wealthy and the poor. People within a society ranked each other according to how much money they had and the type of work they performed. The richest people were considered important, and those with little money were looked down on. A slave was not thought to be significant at all.

Now that slave owners had more free time, they devoted themselves to writing essays, discussing philosophy, and participating in government. Using your mind to create new ideas was considered to be the highest occupation. Working with your hands was seen as the lowest.

Being a slave or living free did not always last a lifetime. A free person could be captured in war or kidnapped and sold into slavery. And slaves could always hope that they might earn money to buy their freedom or that their master might grant them freedom.

## Even Children Were Slaves

Children born to slaves became the property of the mother's owner. A master usually did not sell children away from their mothers, although he could. A child could be trained to sing, dance, play an instrument, or cook meals. The young slave grew in value as he grew older, and if he was eventually sold, the owner earned a great profit.

## Exodus

In a dramatic example of escaped slaves, Moses led the Hebrew people out of bondage in Egypt. After the Israelites had been enslaved for about 350 years, Moses warned the pharaoh that God would send a plague upon the Egyptians if the Israelites were not set free. After ten plagues reportedly struck the Egyptians, the pharaoh allowed Moses to lead the Israelites out. When Moses and the Israelites reached the banks of the Sea of Reeds, the pharaoh ordered his army to recapture them. It is said in the Bible's Book of Exodus that Moses pointed his walking staff at the water, and the seas parted. The Israelites arrived safely on the opposite shore. When the pharaoh's army followed, the waters closed, and the soldiers drowned.

But many slaves became desperate and tried to run away. This was a risky choice, and not often successful. A runaway was severely punished if caught and might even be kept in chains. Some slaves killed themselves, preferring death to a life of bondage.

In spite of the general attitude that slaves were property, warm relationships of affection and loyalty often developed between household slaves and the families who owned them. However, slave owners could not change the fact that all human beings have feelings and the desire to control their own lives. In early civilizations, slavery was accepted as a normal part of everyday life. But over a long period of time, people finally realized that slavery was cruel.

Pergamum
o Sardis

Ephesus

LYDIA

RHODES

MEDITERRANEAN

SEA

CYPRUS

HITTITES

TAURUS MTS.

Orontes R.

Kaddish

Karchemish

Euphrates

ARMENIA

Mt. Ararat

LAKE VAN

ZAGROS

Great Zab

Lesser Zab

Nineveh

Assur

Tigris

River

MEDIA

RISIN SUN

CASPIAN

ASSYRIA

KASSITES

Sidon
Tyre
Damascus
Palmyra
Megiddo
Jordan River
Jerusalem
Dead Sea
Gaza

Mt Lebanon

Alexandria
Pelusium

Gizeh
Memphis

Lake Fayoum

EGYPT

RIVER

SINAI

Mt Sinai

Abydos

Oasis
of
Amon

Karnak
Thebes
Luxor
1st Cataract

A R A B I A

D E S E R T

Agade
Babylon
BABYLONIA
ELAMITES
Susa

Eridu
Ur
CHALDEES

PERSIAN GULF

*Mesopotamia, Greek for "between the rivers," was located between and around the Tigris and Euphrates rivers, shown on this map.*

Mecca

limit NILE
of the Egyptian Empire
under Usertesen

ETHIOPIA

## Chapter Two

# Captives in Sumer

Some time around 4000 B.C., people settled in the fertile lands between the Tigris and Euphrates rivers. Several ancient civilizations took root where Iraq, Eastern Syria, and southeast Turkey now lie. At first, there were many small city-states, each with its own rulers and gods. The rulers were often at war with each other to gain more land and power. In later times, this area was called Meso-potamia, a name that referred to the location rather than the civilizations that rose to greatness and then fell as new nations took power and prospered.

Probably the earliest known people living in Mesopotamia were the Sumerians. For thousands of years, they farmed the lands irrigated by the rivers around them, and their culture and civilization grew in importance. Some of their city-states were named Ur, Larsa, Lagash, Babylon, and Nippur. By 3000 B.C., Sumerian society was thriving.

## Stories Left Behind

In the nineteenth century, when archaeologists began excavating the remains of these long-buried cities, they discovered clay and stone tablets on which Sumerians had written their history and laws. They used a system of wedge-shaped symbols called **cuneiform writing**. Once archaeologists learned to read the symbols, they were able to study the people's way of life.

They learned that Sumerians had a sophisticated system of slavery. They had the first agricultural society we know of that used so many prisoners of war to work the fields. From the records, we also know that Sumerians kidnapped and enslaved people from neighboring areas.

Sumer had a system in which farmers and small businessmen could borrow gold or silver at high interest rates. If the crops failed, or if business was poor, these debtors couldn't pay back their loans. Sometimes the debtor agreed to become the lender's slave to work off the money owed. If a man died in

18

debt, his entire family could be enslaved and would have to work until the money was repaid.

Scientists also studied remains found in graves to learn more about Sumerian society. In the kingdom of Ur, the burial

*People living in the kingdom of Ur worshiped in temples similar to this one.*

site of one ruler contained rich ceremonial clothing, weapons, and the bodies of some of the king's wives. The tomb also held the remains of several slaves who probably drank a special poison that put them into a deep sleep from which they never awoke. Archaeologists believe they died willingly in order to follow their king and serve him in the afterlife.

A special god protected each city-state in Sumer, and a ruler-priest governed each one. Below the ruler were three general groups, or **classes**, of people. The highest class included priests, soldiers, and wealthy nobles. They didn't farm land, but they received a portion of the harvest. Next on the social scale came a large middle class of businessmen, traders, craftsmen, and professionals who worked in medicine

and law. Also in this group were **scribes**, well-educated young men and women who had attended temple schools and learned to read, write, and use advanced math. They held important jobs that required these skills. At the bottom of the society were slaves, who performed all the difficult and menial tasks others demanded of them.

## Slaves Build, Dig, and Work

Slaves made hundreds of thousands of mud bricks and constructed the buildings that dominated the towns. Sumerians built great temples to honor their gods and huge palaces for their rulers—all with slave labor.

*Modern-day canals are not much different from the canals built in Sumer six thousand years ago.*

An extensive system of irrigation canals was one of the foundations of Sumerian civilization. The canals were needed to control the seasonal floods that would otherwise have destroyed their crops. These canals probably date as far back as 4000 B.C. and were certainly dug out with the backbreaking labor of slaves. Other slaves cared for farm animals or planted and harvested the wheat, corn, barley, dates, figs, and vegetables that fed the people. They ground grain into flour, cooked and served meals, cleaned homes, and washed clothes.

Slaves wove the fine woolen cloth that draped their masters and mistresses. The lords and ladies of the house wore garments that covered one shoulder and fell below their knees. Sandals or soft leather shoes made by slaves protected their feet. But servants went barefoot and wore only a rough garment tied around their waists when working in the house.

While the educated upper classes wrote laws, studied astronomy, and developed mathematics, the slaves created beautiful gold and silver objects to decorate their masters' homes and adorn their bodies with jewelry. Slaves also made the shields and weapons used in battles so that Sumerian soldiers could capture more slaves.

## Slaves for Sale

When a neighboring city-state was captured, all its people could be enslaved. If there were too many prisoners to sell at a good profit, soldiers slaughtered many of them. Captives who had operated businesses of their own or were skilled in

cooking, baking, pottery, or weaving continued to work at their trade, but now they were forced to do it for a master. Any children born to a slave automatically became slaves for life.

By 2000 B.C., the Sumerians made payments with silver coins called **shekels**. A healthy male slave sold for about 11 shekels, the same price as a small plot of land. It was considered a high cost.

*This illustration shows the front and back of a silver shekel, which was used for money.*

## Paths to Freedom

Sometimes, free men or women married a slave and granted their new spouse freedom. Any children born in this marriage were considered to be free.

Women in Sumerian society were given more opportunity to work at a business and handle money than in most other

*Women could buy or sell slaves, such as these shown working in the fields.*

early civilizations. After her wedding, a woman decided how she would use her **dowry,** the money and goods given by her family as part of the marriage arrangement. She could use these funds to buy servants, and she could sell or free her slaves whenever she chose.

But women were never considered equal to men. A man had power over his wife and children, because he was considered their legal owner. For example, he could sell any member of his family into slavery to pay a debt.

It was never easy for a slave to run away. If his home city had been captured, where could he go? Even worse, slaves in Sumer were branded with a hot iron like cattle. A symbol or a name identifying the owner was placed where it could easily be seen, such as on the hand or the arm. It was a crime to hide or remove the brand. Slaves also had a leather cord tied around their necks with a clay tablet attached. The tablet listed the slave's name and the name of his master.

After winning a battle, the ruler gave out large parcels of land to victorious generals and favorite nobles. When their slaves farmed these additional lands for them, these men grew even richer. The more slaves a man owned, the greater his status.

Often, masters would choose spouses for their slaves. Slave couples were not officially married. Any children born to them increased the number of slaves masters owned. They could also make a profit by selling the children, but owners usually didn't take slave children from their families.

For thousands of years, Sumer dominated the lands of Mesopotamia. Its growth and prosperity were based largely on the work of slaves.

*Many statues have been found of Hammurabi, a famous king of Babylon.*

## Chapter Three

# Babylonia and Assyria

As with other ancient civilizations, Sumer's dominance did not last. By 2000 B.C., the city-state of Babylon had grown powerful and successfully attacked its neighbors. Beginning in 1792 B.C., King Hammurabi ruled. He was a brilliant and fearless military leader. Within ten years he had captured neighboring lands and created the Babylonian Empire.

Hammurabi knew the laws and science the Sumerians had developed, and he built upon their knowledge and went far beyond them. He promoted the studies of mathematics and astronomy, and fostered great progress in medicine, physics, literature, and philosophy. Under his rule, Babylonian civilization reached its peak.

## The Code of Hammurabi

Perhaps Hammurabi's greatest achievement was a collection of laws that governed every aspect of life and unified the people he had brought under his rule. He believed he had been given these laws by the sun god, Shamash, to make his people's lives safer. The Code of Hammurabi was carved into large stone tablets called **stelae**, and set into the front of temples throughout his empire. The code governed every level of society, from nobles to commoners to slaves, and concerned property, business, injuries, employment, and family responsibilities. The 285 laws set harsh punishments for anyone who broke them.

Many of the laws dealt with the ownership of slaves. Although Hammurabi didn't abolish slavery, he tried to make sure that slaves would be treated decently. He made it illegal for any master to kill a slave or injure another man's slave. He decreed that no debtor could be held in bondage longer than four years. He also made it legal for owners to pay slaves a small wage and established rules that allowed slaves to buy their own freedom.

Under Babylonian law, slaves who saved enough money could purchase cattle or other property, and even own another

## Carved in Stone

A stone cylinder with the Code of Hammurabi was
unearthed in 1902. It is now in the Louvre Museum in Paris.

slave. A slave with special skills might run his own business, if his master wished to invest in setting it up. The slave then gave a large portion of his earnings to his owner, but was allowed to keep some for himself. If he was successful, he might save enough to buy his freedom. But this was difficult to do, and didn't happen often.

Laws about runaways were harsh. A recaptured slave could be kept in shackles or put to death. Anyone who hid a fugitive slave was heavily fined, but if a free man returned a runaway slave, he earned a reward.

Babylonian slaves could be drafted into the army at any time. The king might also draft a free man, but a slave owner called into service could simply send a slave to take his place.

## How Slaves Were Treated

Men and women captured in wars increased the slave population. Also, pirates attacked ships navigating on the rivers, plundered them for goods, and sold the passengers into slavery in Babylonia. Slaves built the roads, bridges, and canals the empire needed. Many farmed the land alongside peasants. Others were given as tribute to the temples. There they produced food for the priests and maintained the buildings. Priests rented out some slaves to others and kept the money they earned for the temple.

Slaves in Babylonia could be easily identified. While their masters wore turbans and their mistresses had elaborate hairstyles, a slave's head was shaved. Masters provided their ser-

### Slaves Take Over the Population

Babylonian society was so dependent on slave labor that eventually the empire had more slaves than free citizens.

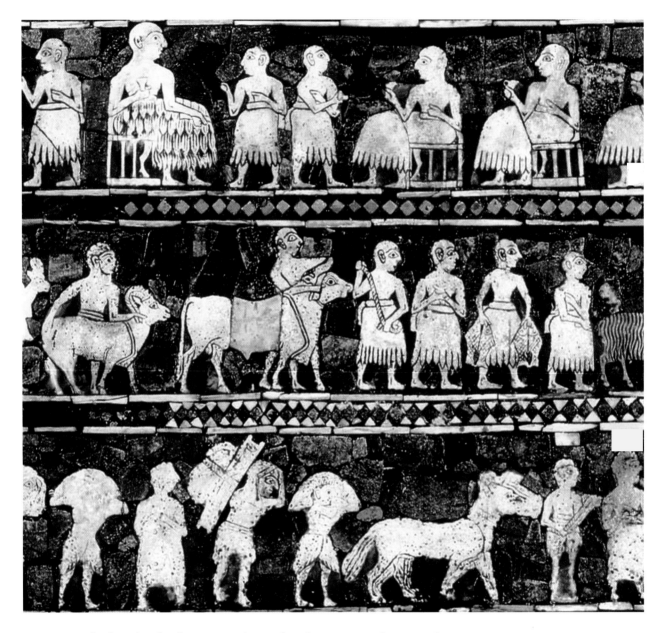

vants with food, clothing, and medical care, and gave them a place to live. But these basic necessities didn't have to be generous. Some owners treated their household slaves as part of the family, while others gave them only enough food to keep

*This mosaic shows Babylonian slaves doing a variety of jobs.*

them alive. Generally, a master kept a slave for a lifetime, even when the slave was too old or too ill to work. Sometimes, a master's will stated that a slave was to be freed. On rare occasions, a master granted his slave freedom for performing some extraordinary service, such as saving the owner's life.

## Rise of Assyria

About 300 miles (483 kilometers) north of Babylon, along the Tigris River, another city-state rose to prominence. In 746 B.C., Tiglath-pileser III became ruler of Assyria and fought bat-

*This picture shows the reception hall of an Assyrian palace.*

tles to regain some of the Assyrian lands that had been lost earlier. With the city of Nineveh as its center, the kingdom of Assyria controlled a great stretch of Mesopotamia. Each spring, its armies launched wars against its neighbors, capturing their cities, looting their gold, silver, and grain, and enslaving their citizens.

King Sennacherib of Assyria's murderous army wore iron armor and traveled with cavalry, as well as chariots and foot soldiers. The capture of Babylon was one of Sennacherib's greatest victories. He burned the city and killed nearly all its

residents. Assyria soon expanded its borders to include the lands of Egypt. Victorious generals gave some of their looted treasure to officers and soldiers—from gold and silver to prisoners of war who could be sold or kept as slaves.

Assyria had five classes of people. The highest group included priests and nobles. Next came free **artisans**, who were highly skilled craftsmen and artists. Then came unskilled free men, who worked for others for pay, and peasants who farmed their own small plot of land. Below them, **serfs** were free men who lived and worked on wealthy landowners' vast estates, but were never permitted to leave the land. Below them all were slaves.

Slaves in Assyria were not branded, but like their Babylonian counterparts, their heads were shaved. They also had pierced ears to identify them. Slaves performed menial tasks for their masters and were often treated cruelly.

## Babylonia Rises Again

Despite its defeat at the hands of the warlike Assyrians, Babylonia rose against its Assyrian rulers and once again became the most powerful force in Mesopotamia. Babylonia continued to wage wars against neighboring states, traveling farther away and enslaving tens of thousands of people.

In 605 B.C., hundreds of years after Hammurabi ruled, Nebuchadrezzar II ascended the throne of Babylonia. He began a massive building campaign to protect the city and honor the gods—and himself. He rebuilt the temple of Marduk, which had been ruined by the Assyrians. Slaves baked mud bricks by the millions and constructed temples and palaces. Every brick made during the king's rule was inscribed with the message, "I am Nebuchadrezzar, King of Babylon." To enhance the beauty of these massive structures, slaves painted glazed tiles with colorful birds, flowers, and animals, and placed them on the outside of the buildings.

To protect the city from invaders, the king had slaves and peasants build a massive wall 56 miles (90 km) around. Some say the wall was so thick that a soldier could drive his chariot along the top.

## Tower of Babel

High atop a hill, Nebuchadrezzar built a towering temple called a **ziggurat**. Its seven levels rose 650 feet (198 meters) toward the heavens. To build it, slaves stood on wooden scaffolding, raised the bricks, and decorated them with enameled tiles. They topped the crown of the ziggurat with a shrine-filled room decorated in gold. A winding stairway snaked around the outside of the tower. Later, this structure was described in the Old Testament story of the Tower of Babel. In the Bible story, God caused the builders to suddenly speak in different languages. We now think of the word *babble* to describe meaningless words or sounds, but it actually refers to Babylon, and means "Gate of God."

*The Hanging Gardens of Babylon no longer exist, but this picture shows what they might have looked like.*

The most amazing structure was the Hanging Gardens that Nebuchadrezzar built to please one of his wives. The Greeks named it one of the Seven Wonders of the World. The gardens were built on tall columns high above the king's most elaborate palace. Rich soil was carted in to fill terraced steps. The gardens overlooked the dry desert and bloomed with exotic flowers, plants, vines, and trees. Hydraulic engines,

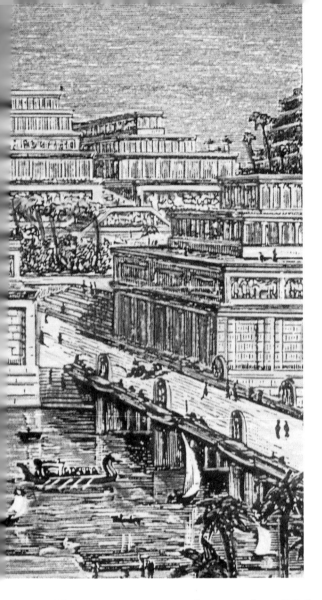

powered by water pressure, pumped water from the Euphrates River. Slaves worked day and night to carry the water to thirsty greenery.

Its temples, palaces, and ziggurats made Babylon the richest city the ancient world had known. Many people forgot that slave labor produced its monuments and its riches.

In 597 B.C., Babylonian forces captured the city of Jerusalem, and they took three thousand Hebrews as slaves. About ten years later, the Hebrews who remained in Jerusalem rebelled, but were brutally defeated. The victorious Babylonians enslaved the surviving Hebrews and took them to Mesopotamian lands. Modern Jewish historians refer to this period as "The Great Captivity." It lasted nearly fifty years, until Persia captured Babylonia and granted the Hebrews freedom to return to their own land.

*The Egyptians recorded their history on tombs and temples with hieroglyphics.*

## Chapter Four

# Pharaoh's Slaves

The land of Egypt was founded around 3000 B.C. where the valley and delta regions of the Nile River united. The Nile River provided a transportation route, as well as a dependable source of water to irrigate crops.

Because the climate was so dry, many Egyptian monuments, homes, and everyday items were preserved over many centuries. **Hieroglyphs**, picture symbols representing sounds, were carved on tombs and temples. These symbols gave

*The Egyptian pharaoh owned many slaves.*

archaeologists a written record of Egyptian history. A pharaoh and his queen ruled the country, and the people believed their rulers were descended from the gods. The pharaoh owned the land, its resources, and its people.

Unlike the empires in Mesopotamia where individuals owned many slaves, in Egypt, the pharaoh owned them all. Free men couldn't buy slaves, but the ruler might give them to some citizens. Others were given to victorious generals as a reward. As in other countries of the time, slaves were usually criminals or war captives.

As Egypt conquered new lands, generals plundered huge quantities of riches and took many prisoners. Before being led away, captives' arms were tied behind their backs and they were attached to each other with long lengths of rope. Some had wooden handcuffs fastened to their wrists. Cloth slings bound babies to their mothers' backs. Slaves generally wore only a loincloth around their waist. In early times, this was similar to the clothing worn by their masters.

The pharaoh decided where each slave would work. Some male slaves had to serve in the army. Educated slaves and those with special skills worked in the palace. They ran government offices, collected taxes, advised the ruler, or created beautiful objects to decorate temples and palaces. Other slaves cooked, wove cloth, sewed clothes, or worked in the fields. Servants who were given to nobles and priests could be assigned any task, from doing personal chores and household labor to running a large business.

One of the most difficult jobs for a slave was working to build a massive monument to honor the pharaoh, or a temple dedicated to the gods. Thousands of slaves spent their entire lives dragging stone blocks weighing several tons each along

## Temple Slaves

During his reign from 1204-1172 B.C., the Pharaoh Ramses III gave temple priests 113,000 slaves.

*Slaves built the Pyramids of Giza in Egypt.*

hundreds of miles of specially built roads. These blocks were used to construct the pyramids. Because slave labor was plentiful, the Egyptians never developed machines that might have moved the stones more easily.

Working in gold mines was at least as fearsome as construction. Naked slaves mined for long hours under horrible conditions. Men worked deep underground hacking at the gold **ore**, rocks that contained the precious metal. Children

## Stone by Stone

The word *pyramid* comes from an Egyptian word meaning "altitude." The pyramids rose some 500 feet (152 m) from the desert sand. The Greek historian Herodotus said it took 100,000 workers 20 years to build the Pyramids of Giza. At the Pyramid of Khufu, workers hauled 2.5 million stones, each averaging 2.5 tons. As part of their taxes, peasants left their farms to work on pyramids in three-month shifts. Slaves worked on them all their lives.

*This illustration shows Egyptians smelting and working gold-bearing ore.*

carried the stones up in baskets, and women and the elderly washed the ore. Slave miners' lives were so unbearable that it is thought that many wished for an early death to release them.

## Peasants Are Taxed with Labor

The Egyptian economy was different from other systems in the region because slave labor was never essential. The ruler could command anyone to work on his projects without payment.

The pharaoh gave to his noblemen large tracts of land, along with the peasants who lived on them. Peasants were free people who planted and harvested crops, tended orchards, or raised sheep, cattle, goats, and pigs. They had to give a large portion of every crop to the noble who owned the land.

Peasants didn't serve in the army, since their labor was needed to produce food. However, after the crops were harvested, the pharaoh demanded that they work on public projects. This was a form of taxation in which people owed service, rather than money. Forced work by free men was called **corvée** labor. Peasants helped build the huge pyramids that served as the pharaohs' tombs. They also constructed and maintained temples, canals, and dikes that kept the Nile from flooding the fields during rainy seasons.

Despite its wealth and resources, Egypt, too, was eventually conquered. In 48 B.C., the Roman emperor Julius Caesar captured the principal city of Alexandria, and within twenty years, Egypt's greatness was history, its lands just another province of Rome.

The caravan of
Abraham traveled
many miles.

## Chapter Five

# Slavery in Hebrew Society

In the Bible, the Book of Genesis (11:31) tells the story of how Abraham, the father of the Hebrew people, traveled with his family from Sumer to Canaan (Palestine). Abraham's descendants split into several nomadic tribes. They called themselves Israelites and were shepherds, artisans, and merchants.

Around 1700 B.C., a long drought in Canaan threatened widespread famine. At the request of the Israelites, the pharaoh granted them permission to settle in Egypt, where fields were fertile, and there was grazing land for their sheep and goats. They moved into the Nile delta and lived there peacefully for about 150 years.

## Slaves in Egypt

Around 1550 B.C., a new pharaoh decreed that all foreigners living on Egyptian lands were his slaves. Tens of thousands of people from many countries were forbidden to leave. The Israelites became part of a large slave class forced to build cities and pyramids. This era lasted until around 1200 B.C., when Moses finally led his people across the Sea of Reeds and out of captivity.

The Hebrew people used Moses' religious teachings as the basis for their civil law. Moses said that God dictated the laws. The laws are written in the first five books of the Bible, which the Hebrews called the **Torah**. Israelite priests interpreted the laws, made judgments, and enforced them.

As in every country in the known world at this time, citizens in Canaan owned slaves who were mostly prisoners of war or con-

## Life of Moses

Moses was born to a family of Israelites during a period when the pharaoh decreed the death of all newborn Hebrew sons. According to the Old Testament, Moses' mother placed him in a reed basket and floated him down the Nile River, where he was found and adopted by one of the pharaoh's daughters and raised in the palace. Moses' mother became his nursemaid and taught him about his own people. As an adult, he killed an overseer who was beating an Israelite slave. He then had to flee from Egypt. The Book of Genesis says that many years later, God spoke to Moses and told him to return and convince the pharaoh to free the Israelites and lead them back to Canaan. After God sent ten plagues to frighten the Egyptians, the pharaoh finally agreed to let the Israelites go. During forty years of wandering the desert, Moses convinced many of his people to believe in one god and helped prepare the Israelites to recapture their land in Canaan.

*This picture shows slaves rebuilding Solomon's temple.*

victed criminals. Israelite men felt they had to own at least a few household slaves, since it was considered immoral for their wives and daughters to go to public wells to collect water or travel to the city's shared ovens to bake the family's bread.

Some slaves worked on public projects. Many labored to build an elaborate temple for King Solomon, who was known for both his wisdom and his elegant palaces. The slaves cut down trees and carted lumber and other materials over long distances. It took nearly eight years for slaves to construct the temple and create the works of art that decorated its rooms.

As in other countries, some free men paid their debts by offering themselves as slaves. The priests eventually ruled that these **bondmen** must be hired as paid servants, and that any debt should be considered repaid within six years.

## How Slaves Were Treated

Unlike in other early civilizations, Israelite masters had only limited power over their slaves. If any master caused a slave physical harm, his slave was immediately granted freedom. If an owner killed a slave, that master was sentenced to death. It was considered cruel to separate slave husbands from wives, or parents from children, and this was never done. Each week on the Sabbath, every person in Canaan, whether slave or free, had a day of rest.

Hebrew priests taught that a master must always speak kindly and listen respectfully to his slave. They encouraged people to free a slave as an act of charity, since no slave had earned the condition in which he found himself. Priests reminded masters not to forget that the Israelite people had once been enslaved in Babylonia and in Egypt.

Slaves in Canaan were allowed to earn money, purchase property, and buy their freedom. A slave who converted to the Hebrew religion was freed, according to Torah law. Also, Hebrews would never sell another Hebrew to a foreigner. Many slave owners granted all their slaves freedom in their wills. If a slave ran away, Hebrews encouraged free men to shelter the runaway, treat him with respect, and not return him.

**Let All Slaves Be Freed**

Based on a passage in the Bible, the Israelites declared a **Jubilee** once every fifty years, during which all slaves were set free.

51

**Ransom for Countrymen**

It was a sacred duty for all Israelites to donate money to a fund used to ransom their captured countrymen.

Slaves in Israelite households were usually treated as part of the family. They might be adopted and were often granted freedom as an act of kindness. Slaves who were acquired at a young age or were born into slavery in the household were raised much the same as the family's own children. They were given the same food and education, and the master arranged a favorable marriage for them. Slaves often looked upon their master as if he were their father and mourned him when he died. Slaves who converted and married a Hebrew were accepted in society, and there was no prejudice against people of other races.

# Where Slavery Was Forbidden

As far as we know, only two areas in the ancient world were free of slavery. These were Hebrew communities whose laws forbade slavery. This was an extraordinary ruling in those days. One group was called the Essenes. They lived near the Dead Sea at the end of the first century B.C. and preached against war, violence, and social injustice of all kinds.

The second group, the Therapeutae, lived near the city of Alexandria. They believed that slavery was against the law of nature. They preached that no human should hold another human in bondage.

The ideas held by these Hebrew societies were rare in the ancient world. It was many centuries before their views were widely accepted and slavery was finally abolished.

# Timeline

| | |
|---|---|
| 4000 B.C. | City-states are formed in an area of Mesopotamia. |
| 3000 B.C. | Peak of civilization is reached in Sumer. |
| 3000 B.C. | Egypt is founded. |
| 2000 B.C. | Babylonia rises to dominance in Mesopotamia. |
| 1792 B.C. | Hammurabi rules Babylonia. |
| 1700 B.C. | Israelites (Hebrews) settle in Egypt. |
| 1550 B.C. | Egypt enslaves all foreigners in its lands. |
| 1200 B.C. | Moses leads Israelites out of bondage in Egypt. |
| 732 B.C. | Assyria rises to prominence in Mesopotamia. |
| 705–681 B.C. | Sennacherib rules Assyria. |
| 674 B.C. | Assyria occupies Egypt. |
| 625 B.C. | Babylonia returns to power in region. |
| 612 B.C. | Assyria falls from power in Mesopotamia. |
| 605 B.C. | Nebuchadrezzar II rules Babylonia. |
| 568 B.C. | Nebuchadrezzar II invades Egypt. |
| Circa 90 B.C. | Essenes and Therapeutae societies ban slavery. |

# Glossary

**artisan**—a skilled craftsman or artist

**bondage**—a state of slavery or forced servitude

**bondman**—a slave or serf

**city-state**—a large city and its surrounding territory, ruled by one strong government

**classes**—different groups of people in a society who were ranked according to birth, wealth, or other status

**corvée**—forced work demanded by a ruler from free men as part of their tax payment

**cuneiform writing**—a system of wedge-shaped symbols that the Sumerians carved into clay and stone tablets to record their history and culture

**debtor**—a person who owed money to other people

**dowry**—the money and goods a woman's family gave when she married

**hieroglyph**—a symbol used by the Egyptians to record their history and laws

**Jubilee**—a special day described in the Bible on which all Hebrew slaves were set free; the celebration occurred once every fifty years

**nomad**—a person who moved from one location to another, instead of settling permanently in one area

**ore**—a mineral rock that contains a metal, such as gold, silver, or bronze

**philosopher**—a person who studies ideas of truth and values

**scribe**—a member of an early civilization who was taught to read and write in order to record documents and events

**serf**—a free person who worked on the farm of a wealthy landowner and were not permitted to leave the land

**shekel**—an early form of money

**stele**—a large stone tablet recording an event or a law

**Torah**—the first five books of the Old Testament Bible, containing Hebrew religious laws and literature

**ziggurat**—a towering temple, wider at the bottom and narrower at the top, built by Assyrians and Babylonians

# To Find Out More

## Books

Coote, Roger. *Ancient Civilizations*. New York: Smithmark Publishers Inc., 1992

Koenig, Viviane, and Veronique A. Georges. *The Ancient Egyptians*. Brookfield, CT: Millbrook Press, 1992.

Meltzer, Milton. *All Times, All Peoples: A World History of Slavery*. New York: Harper and Row, 1980.

*What Life Was Like on the Banks of the Nile*. Alexandria, VA: Time-Life Books, 1996.

Millard, Anne. *How People Lived*. London: Dorling Kindersley, 1993.

# Organizations and Online Sites

Ancient Egypt

*http://www.ancientegypt.co.uk/menu.html*

Visitors to this site can learn more about many aspects of Egyptian life, including gods and goddesses, trades, and writing.

The Carnegie Museum of Natural History

4400 Forbes Ave.

Pittsburgh, PA 15213

*http://www.clpgh.org/cmnh/exhibits/index.html*

The museum offers a special online exhibit of life in ancient Egypt where visitors can learn more about Egyptian daily life.

The Metropolitan Museum of Art

1000 Fifth Avenue at 82nd Street

New York, NY 10028-0198

*http://www.metmuseum.org/*

The museum displays thousands of artworks and artifacts from many historical periods and regions, including ancient Assyria and Egypt.

Odyssey Online

*http://www.emory.edu/CARLOS/ODYSSEY/*

This site provides visitors with information, images, maps, and games about ancient Egypt and other ancient cultures.

Oriental Institute Museum
1155 East 58th Street
Chicago, Illinois 60637
*http://www-oi.uchicago.edu/OI/default.html*
The museum contains many artifacts from ancient Egypt, Mesopotamia, and Assyria that visitors can view online.

The Seven Wonders of the Ancient World
*http://ce.eng.usf.edu/pharos/wonders/*
This site provides the history and images of the Seven Wonders of the Ancient World, including the Egyptian pyramids and the Hanging Gardens of Babylon.

# A Note on Sources

I read more than dozen books to research the topic of slavery in ancient civilizations. I took notes on more than 250 note cards and then organized them by topic before I sat down to write. Two books, *Slavery: From the Rise of Civilization to the Renaissance*, by Milton Meltzer, and *The History of Slavery*, by Norman Macht, were most useful for basic information about early slave life.

The books I most enjoyed using were part of a large set of books called *The Story of Civilization*, written in 1954 by a famous historian, Will Durant. This set of books was filled with fascinating descriptions of each early civilization, and depictions of the people's lives written in a highly readable style. I found many interesting details and tidbits in this volume and spent many hours lost in its pages, envisioning life in a bygone time.

—*Jacqueline Dembar Greene*

# Index

Numbers in *italics* indicate illustrations.

# About the Author

**Jacqueline Dembar Greene** has always been interested in creating stories about people living in past times. She has written numerous fiction and nonfiction books telling stories of characters living in a time and place far removed from our own. Her picture book, *Butchers and Bakers, Rabbis and Kings*, set in Spain in 1114, was a finalist for the National Jewish Book Award. Her historical novels, *Out of Many Waters*, and *One Foot Ashore*, set in 1654, were both named Sydney Taylor Honor Books.

Ms. Greene has traveled throughout the southwestern United States, Mexico, Europe, and Russia. She has used her experiences and photographs as background in writing several nonfiction books for Franklin Watts, including *The Maya*, *The Chippewa*, *The Tohono O'odham*, and *Powwow: A Good Day to Dance*.